AMAZING GRACE

AMAZING GRACE

GRACE INFINIE

Evangelist Roseline N. Turenne

ARPress

ILLUMINATING IDEAS,
EMPOWERING VOICES

ARPress
45 Dan Road Suite 36
Canton MA 02021
Hotline: 1(888) 821-0229
Fax: 1(508) 545-7580

Ordering Information:
Quantity Sales. Special discounts are available on quantity purchases by corporations, associations, and others. For details, contact the publisher at the address above.

Printed in the United States of America.

ISBN-13   Paperback   979-8-89330-324-7
             eBook   979-8-89330-325-4

Library of Congress Control Number: 2024900480

Table Of Contents

Dedication

I dedicated my book to my Heavenly Father who gave me knowledge and understanding to write my second book. I humbly bow before you Lord in Jesus mighty name.

I dedicated my book to my dearly husband Oglanda Turenne who always encourages me to do the Lord ministry in good times and in bad times always there with me. I love you so much.

I dedicated my book to my mother Jeanne Mariette Calixte who always prays for me and encourages me to go forward. I thank God for her and my second mother Lunise Auguste. May the Lord bless you all.

I dedicated my book to my brother Lochard Noel and his wife Elizabeth Noel. And my sister Yolette Noel Cayo and her husband Edner Cayo.

I dedicated my book to my nephew Pastor Jean Marie Louis and his wife Chimene Louis and my nephew Hansy Louis and his wife Natasha Louis and my niece Colette Cok and her husband Derocher Cok and my spiritual daughter Jomara Leonard.

May The Lord bless you all.

Acknowledgements

I dedicated my book to my Pastor Rev. Dr. Jacques Nicolas and his wife Françoise Nicolas.

Pastor Remy Almonord, Pastor Baptiste Jean- Pierre.

Pastor Yves Mildort and his wife Marie Ange Mildort and Pastor Yves Mildort the second.

Pastor Iserael Pigne and his wife Marie Pigne. Pastor Abner Noel and his wife Evangelist Roselaine Noel. Pastor Offrande Auguste. Pastor Pierre Clermont. Major Metelus Charles and his wife Major Adeline Charles.

Brother Abedef Metellus. Pastor Pierre Pietro Malbranche and his wife Shell Milien-Malbranche. Maestro Ludas Charles. Adely Charles. Mozart Charles. Patrick Desroches and his wife Maguy Desroches and Ernsy Jean Chales.

Introduction

In two thousand twelve I do not remember the month and the date, but I truly remember a dream that I had. I saw heaven was very beautiful the blue was extremely brilliant and in the middle of heaven I saw "Amazing Grace" and I saw it in French as well "Grace Infinie" both were written in white color. In the dream I saw some ladies stood up beside me and I said to them you don't see "Amazing Grace" writing in heaven, they said no we do not see it, I continued told them you don't see "Amazing Grace" writing in heaven they said no we don't see it. I continued to say the same thing and they did not see what I saw until I woke up.

This is the reason I say let me write a book about the **"Amazing Grace"** and I know the book is going to touch everyone who read it in Jesus Mighty Name.

I want to remind myself and readers of the book.

"Amazing Grace" is will and I want to let you know as well, Heaven is will.

Please enjoy **"The Amazing Grace"**

Chapter One

The Meaning of Amazing

The New Lexicon Webster's Dictionary defines amazing; it is overwhelmed with wonder amazement.

Urban Dictionary defines amazing as something that is so wonderful. Something that makes your heartbeat faster or your heart melt.

Let us go further to see the meaning of the "Amazing Grace" John Newton the Author of the song "Amazing Grace" stated:

Amazing grace, how sweet the sound…
That saved a wretch like me!
I once was lost, but now am found.
Was blind, but now I see.
'Twas grace that taught my heart to fear,
And grace my fears relieved;
How precious did that grace appear,
The hour I first believed!
Thro' many dangers, toils and snares.
I have already come;
'Tis grace has brought me safe thus far,
And grace will lead me home.
(1725-1807)

This is a deep inspirational song. If I have the privilege to ask John Newton why he wrote this beautiful song he might gave me a lot of reasons why he wrote the song. But story tells us he was a slave, captures for so many years in misery, in tribulation, and humiliation and there was no hope for him until he accepted Jesus Christ as his personal Savior and Lord that is the reason he wrote that beautiful song "Amazing Grace". I truly know everyone has beautiful songs or beautiful books inside of us specially my fellow Christians in the Lord. Sometimes we keep them inside of us. We need to spread them out. Don't be shine, please spread them out. I am not trying to command you but to encourage you because we can do a lot of good things in Jesus Mighty name.

Let us continue to see the meaning of amazing. Amazing has a different definition for so many people but for me, let share to you my definition:

Amazing is something you cannot comprehend and even explain because is to deep for people's knowledge for example the love of God for humanity who can understand and explain that. The bible says, "For God so loved the world that He gave His one and only Son, that whoever believes in Him shall not perish but have eternal life. For God did not send His Son into the world to condemn the world, but to save the world through Him." John three sixteen and seventeen.

God loves every single creature that is amazing wow. The only thing we have to do just accept Him has our personal loving Savior and friend and as well He will be your Father. There is a song writer saying:

"What a friend we have in Jesus
All our sins and griefs to bear!
What a privilege to carry
Everything to
God in prayer!
O what needless pain we bear
All because we do not carry
Everything to God in prayer!"
The love of God is so deep to understand. There is another writer saying:

"What a wonderful change in my life has been wrought
Since Jesus came into my heart.
I have light in my soul for which long I had sought
Since Jesus came into my heart.
Since Jesus came into my heart.
Since Jesus came into my heart,
Floods of joy o'er my soul
Like the sea billows roll.
Since Jesus came into my heart."
Rufus Henry McDaniel (1850-1940)

Has I said before everyone has a different definition or opinion about the amazing. Let us enjoy the amazing love of God. Nothing on this earth can compare the amazing love of God for us. If you do not accept Jesus as your personal Savior, please accept Him because Jesus is the way, the truth, and the life. No one comes to the Father except through me" Stated Jesus to the disciples. (John fourteen verse six b)

It is very amazing to know Jesus is the way, the truth, and the life. No one comes to the Father except through Him.

-What a wonderful, amazing Jesus we have.
Please enjoy the amazing Jesus.

Chapter Two

The Meaning of Grace

What is Grace? Dictionary defines: Grace is a favor rendered by one who needs not do so; indulgence. A temporary immunity or exemption; a reprieve.

Let us go further to see the meaning of grace. When I was a child in my country Haiti when children do something who is not pleasing their parents, they used to beat them up for they wrong doing and the children began to cry and neighbor heard them crying and neighbor came and said grace for he or she and mother or father stop beaten the child and the parents said I give you grace but don't do that anymore.

That is the reason I can come with my own definition "Grace is on merit favor" Readers, I want you to understand the love of God. He had a purpose for each and every one of us. The Bible says, "in the beginning God created the heavens and the earth. Now the earth was formless and empty, darkness was over the surface of the deep, and the Spirit of God was hovering over the waters. And God said, "Let there be light," and there was light. Genesis one verse one to two. Genesis means beginning. God spoke and creation took place I want you to understand has well there is power in word please be careful in what you're saying be positive in word instead of having a negative spirit. We are precious in God sights.

He makes sure He created everything after creations He created us because God did not want us to lack anything on this earth.

After God created us, He gave us power to dominate. Genesis chapter one verse twenty-six stated, then God said, "Let us make man in our image, in our likeness, and let them rule over the fish of the sea and the birds of the air, over the livestock, over all the earth, and over all the creatures that move along the ground."

So God created man in his own image, in the image of God he created him; male and female. So therefore, we are extremely valuable before God. Nothing is new on this earth. Jealousy is a big issue. Everywhere we go we can see the manifestation of jealousy in every area. I have a question, who is the author of jealousy? I know you can answer but let me answer that the enemy is the author of it. He came in the Garden of Eden and lie to Eve saying, "Did God really say, "You must not eat from any tree in the garden?" Genesis chapter three verse one b. We need not to listen to the enemy and that set if we listen to him, we are going to disobey what God say and he will give us the wrong answer and we might listen to him and we are going to be in big trouble. It is better not to listen to any negative voice at all.

Jealousy is a big issue. Our first parent Adam and Eve were so comfortable there was no trouble at all in the garden. When the serpent came everything turned upside down for them. They were naked they did know it until the serpent visited them. The glory of the Lord had covered them they did not naked in the spirit. When the enemy came, they realized they were naked because the glory of the Lord came out of them. Thanks be to God, He gave us a second Adam which is Jesus-Christ of Nazareth who took our Sinful nature and put God on His shoulders. We can boldly say we are saved through the blood of Jesus-Christ. John three sixteen says, "For God so loved the world He gave His one and only Son that whoever believes in Him shall not perish but have eternal life. That is the amazing grace. We cannot explain that because it is too knowledgeable for us to comprehend.

He continues to say but as many as received Him, to them He gave the right to become children of God, to those who believe in His name. John one verse twelve. Grace means we don't need to be perfect to receive forgiveness. Just accept Jesus Christ has your personal Savior and Lord. He paid the penalty for us over two thousand years ago. We are free for every single shameful situation.

5

The book of Romans encourages you to accept Jesus if you don't know Him as your personal Savior and Friend. The word of God says, "If you confess with your mouth the Lord Jesus and believe in your heart that God has raised Him from the dead, you will be saved. Romans ten verse nine.

Amazing grace is will and beautiful. Never hesitate to take Him has your all in all.

Chapter Three

Who we are in Christ

Everyone has an identity, believe it or not. That is the reason each person has an imprint even a trine.

My mother gave me a sad story. She said when she was pregnant her husband did not want her to have a third child and he gave my mother something to drink so she can have an abortion. She did not have a choice not to drink the medicine, because if she did not drink the medicine her husband can beat her up that is the reason she accepted to drink it. Even though she drinks the medicine nothing could stop the baby going up in her womb why because nothing can destroy our special identity.

Who was that beautiful baby Satan wanted to destroy you may ask. I am very happy to answer that question. Not too long ago I learned that story from my mother. My mother has three children, my sister Yolette Noel Cayo, my brother Lochard Noel and I was the third one my father could not accept. When I was born my father accepted me and loved me so very much. My father was born in Santo Domingo when he was about twenty something he came to Haiti and met my mother Jeanne Mariette Calixte. My father did not marry my mother, but my mother told me my father had a nice fiancé with her but for some reason he did not marry my mother. In Haiti they call husband and wife even they not married that is the system long time, but I don't know for now how it is. That is the reason people could not understand who is married or not. Thanks be to God no one can destroy our special identity. We can boldly declare **devil is a liar.**

No one can destroy the plan of God. I am a special tool for the Lord wherever I go. This is the same way for you. Don't be discouraged, God has a plan for your life as well.

The subject is "Who we are in Christ". People love title, isn't it? In my country if you belong to a rich family, they will recognize you and respect you wherever he or she is because you belong to a big, big family.

What about the family of God. Nothing can compare on this earth, because we belong to a great family of God. There is a chorus saying:

> "I'm so glad I'm a part of the Family of God,
> I've been washed in the fountain,
> Cleansed by His Blood!
> Joint heirs with Jesus as we travel His sod,
> For I'm part of the Family,
> The Family of God."
> Author Bill Gaither and Gloria Gaither
> Copyright: 1970, William J. Gaiter, Inc.

We are precious in Jesus mighty name we all belong to the great family of God.

"When we all get to Heaven what a day of rejoicing that will be" I love that song because it is a reality. The family of God will meet together let us start enjoying the moment.

Who we are in Christ? We are valuable, we are precious, and we are beautiful because we belong to the King of kings and the Lord of Lords.

There is now no condemnation for us. Jesus said on the cross before the last word **"It is finished"** John chapter nineteen verse thirty. Which means He took our Penalties, our Shames, our Pains, our Griefs and He set us free.

That is the reason we can boldly say "What a mighty God we serve there is none like Him. No one can take away the love of God and our relationship for us through the blood of Jesus.

Who we are in Christ? We are precious no one can take our special Identity. Thanks be to God. Thank you, Jesus.

Chapter Four

The Christians Roles

W hat is the meaning of Roles? Dictionary defines roles is a character or part played by a performer. Secondly: The characteristics and expected social behavior of an individual. Thirdly: A function or position.

The definition of roles is very large. However, we do have a role to play in every area in our lives. For example, as parents we do have a role to play to educate our children. In our workplace we do have a role to play to do the job properly to keep our job. In our neighborhood we do have a role to play to keep our zone look respectful and beautiful.

What about Christians? – We do have a role to play in so many ways. Our attitude must be different wherever we are. We do not need to tell people all the time we are Christians but by our actions they will recognize us. In church what is our position? Whatever we have to do just do it. We are not doing it for pastor, for bishop, for evangelist, for friend and so one; we are doing it for the Lord and for the Lord only. That is the reason we have to do it properly. Colossians three verse twenty-three and twenty-four says, "Whatever you do, do it heartily, as to the Lord and not to men, knowing that from the Lord you will receive the reward of the inheritance; for you serve the Lord Christ."

We do have a role to play wherever we are. Second Corinthians five verse seventeen must play a big role in our lives.

"Therefore, if anyone is in Christ, he is a new creation; old things have passed away; behold, all things have become new" we are a new creation. We are not the same we used to be, the blood of the lamb washed away our sins. We don't need to be afraid of anything because devil is a liar.

Do not say you cannot do anything, yes you can. You have to claim it just say yes, I can in Jesus Mighty name. We do have a lot of things we can do in church for example: Children ministry, Youth ministry, Ladies ministry, Men ministry, Elderly ministry, Nursing home ministry, Prisons ministry, Missions ministry, Fund raising ministry, Counseling ministry and so one. Just try one you will see how God gone use you. Philippians four thirteen says, "I can do all things through Christ who strengthens me." Try you will see how helpful you going to be for the church and how anointed you are going if you obey the Lord's command. Amen.

Let us keep our responsibility. Sometimes business a little bit slow. Sometimes they even lay off workers because the jobs are very slow. The workers sometimes have to go to social just to get some money to survive. The time is not easy. Business owners can tell. But God is good all the time and all the time God is good.

I was telling about job is not easy to find. But in church there is no market down in church. If you need work, you will find job to do. You might say, I am not qualified to do it. I understand but let me tell you something the only way you are not qualify only if you are not a good example for the church, if you don't have a good attitude, if you do not let the second Corinthians five verse seventeen work in you "Therefore, if anyone is in Christ, he is a new creation; the old has gone, the new has come!"

We do not have any excuse to give. We need to work in the Kingdom of God. I know for Christians, to make it clear, those who accepted Jesus- Christ has personal Savior they are saved through the blood of Jesus-Christ by the Love of God. We need to be useful in the Lord's service, if yes; the Lord is going to reward you with a lot of crowns. There will be a beautiful celebration in Heaven. Do not be lazy find something to do in church not only in church, but also in our community you will see how useful and blessed you are.

11

Our Christians role is to be useful for the Kingdom of God. Please do not be lazy, we all are important in the Kingdom of God.

Chapter Five

The Christians Movements

In everything there is a beginning. That is the reason the first word mentioned in the Bible is "In the beginning" what was going on in the beginning? Let us see, God spoken and things happened. God created heavens and the earth, and He was continued spoken and the whole wide world and us existed today just because God was spoken. My fellow friends and readers please whatever you have in mind to do just do it, take a day to start don't let anyone intimidate you. Just start and never give up. Have faith in God and you will see.

The Christians movements what it is all about? The Gospel of Mark stated, "Later Jesus appeared to the eleven as they were eating; he rebuked them for their lack of faith and their stubborn refusal to believe those who had seen him after he had risen."

He said to them, "Go into all the world and preach the good news to all creation. Whoever believes and is baptized will be saved, but whoever does not believe will be condemned. And these signs will accompany those who believe in my name they will drive out demons; they will pick up snakes with their hands; and when they drink deadly poison, it will not hurt them at all; they will place their hands on sick people, and they will get well." Mark sixteen verses fourteen to eighteen.

Jesus rebuked the disciples for lack of faith not only the disciples but us too. Jesus gave us the order to move to preach the good news into the world, so therefore, we need to move on, we don't need to go to school to evangelize people. We don't need to go to school to lay hands on the sick and so one.

Remember the rules of Christian's movement is to have faith don't let anyone stop you doing God works in Jesus mighty name.

Go and start now!

Chapter Six

The Power of the Church

We always love to see the meaning of the word just to navigate a little bit well, isn't it? That is the reason we need to know what power means. According to dictionary power means ability to act or produce an effect, secondly: Ability to get extra base hits, thirdly: Capacity for being acted upon or undergoing an effect.

Let us see the Bible dictionary definition to see what power is all about: According King James Version Dictionary Power is the faculty of moving or of producing a change in something. Thank God for that beautiful definition.

Isaiah gave us a message he said, "For to us a child is born, To us a son is given, and the government will be on his shoulders. And He will be called <u>Wonderful</u> <u>Counselor</u>, <u>Mighty God</u>, <u>Everlasting Father</u>, and <u>Prince of Peace</u>. Of the increase of His government and peace there will be no end. He will reign on David's throne and over his kingdom, establishing and upholding it with justice and righteousness from that the time on and forever. The zeal of the Lord Almighty will accomplish this," Isaiah nine verse six and seven.

Let us see the meaning of mighty: Dictionary defines mighty: having or showing great power, strength, or force. Prophet Isaiah explained to us a child is born He will be called Wonderful Counselor, Mighty God, Everlasting Father, and Prince of Peace

There, we can boldly say Jesus is the author of Power. That is the reason death could not keep Jesus on the grave because Jesus was too strong for the grave. The reason grave holds Him for three days, because Jesus had His Father's mission to accomplish for the world. Jesus took the key of death in the hand of Satan that is the reason he hates us we don't care anyway. Satan has power but good news Jesus is very powerful. That is the reason Jesus took the key of deception from the hand of Satan, Jesus took the key of humiliation from the hand of Satan so therefore, victory is mine, victory is yours and victory is ours in **Jesus Mighty name!**

The song says: "Would you be free from your burden of sin?
There's power in the blood, power in the blood!
Would you o'er evil a victory win?
There's wonderful power in the blood!
There is power, power, wonder-working power.
In the blood of the Lamb.
There is power, power, wonder-working power,
In the precious blood of the Lamb…"
Words and Music: Lewis Edgar Jones, 1865-1936

Jesus gave the disciples a great commission to spread the power to those who don't know Him. He said to them, "Go into all the world and preach the good news to all creation. Whoever believes and is baptized will be saved, but whoever does not believe will be condemned. Jesus continued to tell the disciples, and these signs will accompany those who believe: in my name they will drive out demons; they will speak in the new tongues; they will pick up snakes with their hands; and when they drink deadly poison, it will not hurt them at all; they will place their hands on sick people, and they will get well. Mark sixteen verse fifteen through eighteen.

The great commission belongs to us today because we are the church and Jesus disciples as well. We don't need to go far away to get power. Jesus anointed us with power already. We just need to believe and receive it. Prayer is the key for power. "My people are destroyed from lack of knowledge." Hosea four verse six. Who are my people? Is the people of God.

The Gospel of Matthew said: "Therefore go and make disciples of all nations, baptizing in the name of the Father and of the Son and of the Holy Spirit, and teaching them to obey everything I have commanded you. And surely, I am with you always, to the very end of the age" Matthew chapter twenty-eight verse twenty.

That is again the Great Commission. Do not let anyone trouble our minds; Jesus gave us the power to lay hands on the sick and they will recover." Jesus did not tell the disciples to lay hands-on sick people and after their recovering they have to pay. Jesus did not tell the disciples to make price when they invite them to preach. Jesus did not teach the disciples to do religious ceremonial activities, for example: To let the people by gallon of water, bottle of oil and handkerchief to receive miracles. Jesus gave us the power; we don't need to buy anything because we have it inside of us. People of God it is time to open our eyes, our minds, our hearts, and our spirits to understand who Jesus is. He said on the cross **"It is finished"** so therefore, we are free from bondage, we are free from poverty, we are free from bad spirit; Jesus is the reality.

Jesus is the power for the church, and He passed the heritage for us, which is Christians today. The church, have power in Jesus name. Who is the church? You and I. Don't let anyone full you. We are not going to perish because from lack of knowledge. We used to do that, but now thanks be to God we do have knowledge. We are free because we know the truth. The church of God please keep the power that you have in Jesus Mighty name. Remember, we have the power, again in Jesus Name.

Jesus said, "Only in his hometown, among his relatives and in his own house is a prophet without honor." (Mark six verse four) that is the reason Church of God is suffering still today. Most of the time they pay much attention to invite people who come very far. But they forget those who have auction among them to do the work because they so familiar with them; be careful leaders not to do that, be careful pastors not to do that, be careful Bishop not to do that, be careful Reverend not to do that, be careful Doctor not to do that, be careful Evangelist not to do that, be careful church not to do that.

17

Remember, Jesus gave us power, it is not a joke, we are the church, and the church means Power because Jesus said so.

Amen and Amen!

Chapter Seven

The Promises of God

W hat is Promises? Webster's dictionary defines a declaration assuring that one will or will not do something; a vow. Something promised. Indication of something favorable to come…

We make a lot of promises for example: to our husbands, wives, children, relatives, friends and so one. When we were married my husband and I made promises to stay together in good and in bad situations that was the wedding vow. Each couple knows what I am talking about. A lot of promises are failed sometimes for some reasons. No matter what, promises are very good to do but to keep them it is not easy. But by the grace of God, we can be successful in our promises.

We love to go to our best book, which is the Bible it is the book of books, yes, it is there, and there is no lie about it. Let us go to see the Bible dictionary first: Promise: An express assurance on which expectation is to be…Bible dictionary.com

The story of Jesus started with a promise. She will give birth to a son, and you are to give him the name Jesus, because he will save his people from their sins. All this took place to fulfill what the Lord had said through the prophet: the virgin will be with child and will give birth to a son, and they will call him Immanuel: which means, **"God with us."** Matthew one verse twenty-one to twenty-three. That is the biggest promise that never existed.

"Immanuel" which means, "God With us" The Promises of God are yes, and amen reason, His name means the true promises He said, I will never leave you; never will I forsake you. (Hebrew thirteen verse two b) If God leave us for one second, we will not be alive. Even the world is very bad still God loves the world anyway because His love is unconditional. The promises of God are never failed.

God said to His disciples, "Do not let your hearts be troubled. Trust in God; trust also in me. Jesus continued to say; "In my Father's house are many rooms; if it were not so I would have told you. I am going there to prepare a place for you. And if I go and prepare a place for you, I will come back and take you to be with me that you also may be where I am. (John fourteen verse one and three) There is no better place than to be with the Master.

The angel of the Lord announced the birth of Jesus as our Savior; He will take away our sins. This is the promise of God through the blood of Jesus Christ. Whosoever shall be saved.

Please don't give up. Stay focus. God has a plan for you and for me. He has a plan for all of us. Don't be afraid. Whatever you have to do just do it. Don't give up on your dream. We know it is not easy. It is easy to destroy than to build. To destroy, just in a few minutes you do it. But to build he will take hours and years to accomplish your dream. Don't listen to the negative voice, I remember I said to someone I have in mind to write a book the negative person told me you can not do it. **Cannot**, not exist in the dictionary of God. Let me tell you something that is my second book in Jesus name.

Husbands and wives, your marriages are beautiful and perfect. Parents your children are very smart and beautiful. Teachers, your students are very intelligent and beautiful. We live in nice neighborhood because we are very beautiful in Jesus mighty name.

Positive thought came from the Bible. Proverb eighteen verses twenty- one stated, "The tongue has the power of life and death, and those who love it will eat its fruit. So therefore, let us start thinking positive we will see how precious it is.

The promises of God are yes and amen. There is a song says,

"Precious promise God has given

To the weary passerby,
On the way from earth to Heaven,
I will guide thee with Mine eye." Refrain
I will guide thee, I will guide thee,
I will guide thee with Mine eye;
On the way from earth to Heaven,
I will guide thee with Mine eye.
When temptations almost with thee
And thy trusted watchers fly,
Let this promised ring within thee,
I will guide thee with Mine eye.
When the secret hopes have perished
In the grave of years gone by,
Let this promise still be cherished,
I will guide thee with Mine eye.
When shades of life are falling
And the hour has come to die,
Hear thy trusty Pilot cling,
I will guide thee with Mine eye."
Wrote by: Nathaniel Niles (1835-1917)

I love the song it is a reality. Don't give up, keep your dream alive – The promises of God are yes and Amen.

Don't let anyone look down on you because you are young or because you are old or because you are black or because you are white or because you are not born in the United States and so one.

Keep your dream alive because the promises of God never expire.

Don't give up on your dream.

The promises of God never fail!

Chapter Eight

What is Heaven?

Heaven is the place where God dwells. It is a location that is wholly spiritual in nature. Christians defines heaven as being in the presence of God with places. According to Dictionary.

As Christians, Heaven means a lot to us. No matter who we are, we all know there is a place that God dwells which is heaven. No matter the people's belief.

There is a young boy when he was three, he was dead and come back to life. I have the opportunity to see him on TBN and I think so many people saw him too. The young boy went to heaven and came back to tell all. The first person he saw was Jesus; Jesus was wearing a white robe. Then, the second person he saw was his father's grandfather. After that he saw his sister, his mother said she had some years ago a miscarriage and his son saw his little sister in heaven. Jesus said to him, "You need to go back, because I answered your father's prayer" the little boy said, "I did not want to go back, Jesus said to him you have to go back tell people what you saw. He wrote a book "Heaven is for real" so many people love to go to heaven even they do not accept Jesus as their personal Savior and Lord; reason, because they know heaven is a safety place. Heaven is real – there is no joke about it.

All Christians, the lover of Jesus Christ know heaven is our sweet home that is the reason Charles Wesley the author of the beautiful song "Heaven came down" expressed himself how heaven is all about to believe we need to have faith because without faith it is impossible to please God. The author stated:

"What a wonderful, wonderful day
Day I will never forget;
After I'd wandered in darkness away,
Jesus my Savior I met!
O what a tender, compassionate friend.
He met the need of my heart!
Shadows dispelling, with joy I am telling
He made all the darkness depart.
Heaven came down and Glory filled my soul.
When at the cross the Saviour made me whole;
My sins were washed a way,
And my night was turned to day,
Heaven came down and Glory filled my soul...."
Now I've hope that will surely endure
After the passing of time.
I have future in Heaven for sure.
There in those mansions sublime.
And it's because of that wonderful day,
When at the cross I believed;
Riches eternal and blessings supernal
From his precious hand I received.
(Charles Wesley 1707-88)

Heaven is real, that is our hope. However, if there is heaven there is hell as well. As I said before so many people even though they are not Christians, but they don't want to go to hell because they know hell is a terrible torment place forever. The gospel of Mark chapter nine verses forty-three to forty-nine stated: "If your hand causes you to sin, cut it off. It is better for you to enter life maimed than with two hands to go into hell, where the fire never goes out. And if your foot causes you to sin, cut it off. It is better for you to enter life crippled than to have two feet and be thrown into hell. And if your eye causes you to sin, pluck it out. It is better for you to enter the kingdom of God with one eye than to have two eyes and be thrown into hell, where "their worm does not die, and the fire is not quenched." Everyone will salt with fire." Heaven is real and hell is real, which one do you prefer? I know you prefer heaven. But to go to heaven you need to accept Jesus as your personal Savior, because Jesus is the way to Heaven.

God made provisions for us in Heaven; we are not going to be anxious for anything. There will be no more sickness, there will be no more death, there will be no more humiliation, there will be no more discrimination, and there will be no more debt because Jesus paid the price for us on Calvary cross.

The author of the song says:

"When we all get to heaven,
What a day of rejoicing that will be!
When we all see Jesus,
We will sing and shout the victory!"

We are precious God even placed the angels to wash over our lives before we go to heaven. For he will command his angels concerning you to guard you in all your ways; they will lift you up in their hands, so that you will not strike your foot against a stone.

Psalms ninety-one verse eleven to twelve

Jesus said to his disciples "Do not let your hearts be trouble. Trust in God; trust also in me. In my Father's house are many rooms; if it were not so, I would have told you. I am going there to prepare a place for you. And if I go and prepare a place for you, I will come back and take you to be with me that you also may be where I am. You know the way to the place where I am going."

John fourteen verses one to four.

There will be no squeezing in heaven we are going to see a lot of rooms. Don't Worry be Happy!

Heaven is real, get ready to enjoy our Sweet Home!

Chapter Nine

The love of Jesus-Christ

The love of Jesus Christ is a lovely chapter I know we are going to enjoy this moment.

We need to see the definition of love. Love has many different meanings to all different types of people. There are many stages of love at different ages and different types of love. The real definition of love/ By Purple Slinky

Let us see another definition of love a deep and tender feeling of affection to a person or persons; an expression of one's love or affection: give Mary my love; a feeling of...

The love of Jesus-Christ is unconditional. What is unconditional? Without conditions or limitations according to dictionary. That is the reason dictionary defines in the Bible's definition of love is the purest of all.

Human love you have to do something to be loved or to be appreciated. For God no problem, He loves us unconditionally, which means the way we are. He does not look at your past or your present. He just loves us. The way we are/you are. But He just wants you to change your attitude or your behavior. He does not want you to stay the way we are. God is a forgiving God. If you confess your sins, He is able to forgive you. You don't' have to spend money or religious activities to receive the forgiveness of the Lord. The only thing you have to do just open your heart freely to Him as your personal Savior and friend.

Apostle Paul described the love of God in the book of first Corinthian chapter thirteen. The tile of the chapter is "The Greatest Gifts" Though I speak with the tongues of men and of angels, but have not love; I have become sounding brass or a clanging cymbal. And though I have the gift of prophecy, and understand all mysteries and all knowledge, and though I have all faith, so that I could remove mountains but have not love, I am nothing. That is the reason we all can truly agree love is the greatest gift.

Apostle Paul continued to described love He said, "love is patient, love is kind, it does not envy, it does not boast, it is not proud, it is not rude, it is not self-seeking. As followers of Jesus Christ, we need to have a loving heart, not proud, not selfish ambition, not a self-seeking, not a statistic proud but a true love.

The bible says for God so love the world that He gave His one and only Son that whoever believes in him shall not perish but have eternal life. (John three verse sixteen)

The love of God is pure; the love of God is perfect. No one can come and give Him lie to anyone. He is the King of kings, and He is the Lord of lords. He is the supreme authority. No one can take away the love He has for us, before the foundation of the world He made provisions for us.

The love of God is limitless in French **"L'Amour de Dieu n'a point de limite"** There is no limit in the love of God for us through the blood of Jesus-Christ. We may have gift of healing, we may have gift of prophecy, we may have gift of speaking in tongue and so one that is very good in the body of Christ. As a matter of fact, Jesus gave them to us to operate for the benefit of the church.

But you know something in heaven there will be no more sickness, there will be no more prophecy, and there will be no more speaking in tongue and so one. Because heaven is a perfect place and a unify place. That is the reason you are going to have a new glorious body, a new universal language and we are not going to have prophecy because we are going to seat with our heavenly father. The only thing we are going to have is love, why? Because **Jesus is Love and love is eternal.**

The apostle of John declared, "Dear friends, let us love one another, for love comes from God. Everyone who loves has been born of God and knows God. Whoever does not love does not know God, because God is love. This is how God showed his love among us: He sent his one and only Son into the world that we might live through him. This is love: not that we loved God, but that he loved us and sent his Son as an atoning sacrifice for our sins. Dear friends, since God so loved us, we also ought to love one another, God; but if we love one another, God lives in us, and his love is made complete in us. (First John four verses seven through twelve).

The love of God is eternal, the love of God is precious, the love of God is limitless, and the love of God is unconditional. Thanks be to God through His Son Jesus-Christ our Savior and our Lord. Jesus shouted on the cross **"It is finished"** that is the reason no one can take away the love of God in us because His love is unconditional.

Please enjoy the love of God through His Son Jesus-Christ.

Chapter Ten

The Author of the Amazing Grace

The owners of some existing things are very important. That is the reason no one can touch them without permission of the owners if yes, it's going to cost a lot of problems and penalties. Because it belongs to somebody. There is no joke about it. That is the reason we strongly believe the amazing grace has a special author. Before that let us see what the Apostle Paul declares in the book of Romans chapter eight verses one and two "Therefore, there is now no condemnation for those who are in Christ Jesus, because through Christ Jesus the law of the Spirit of life set me free from the law of sin and death."

Jesus died and they hang Him on the cross He cried out **"It is finished"** in French **"Tout est accompli"** (John nineteen verse thirty) which means He took out all our sins, all our shames, all our condemnations that is the reason Apostles Paul declared "Now, there is no condemnation for those who believe in Jesus-Christ our Lord and our Savior.

Jesus is the only one who declared, **"It is finished"** no one else can take away sins. As a matter of fact, He left His royal throne and came on this world and lives among men, woman, and children. He fed about five hundred people they did not count woman and children. Thanks be to God now everybody's count in the statistics of Jesus-Christ of Nazareth. Jesus transformed Himself as human just to understand our shames and our humiliations. The word says, "He came to that which was his own, but his own did not receive him. Yet to all who received him, to those who believed in his name, he gave the right to become children of God. (John, one verses eleven to twelve). We belong to the King of kings and the Lord of lords is it really amazing isn't't' it? Oh Yes. The apostles of Paul again say, "It is by grace you have been saved, through faith and this not from yourselves, it is the gift of God. (Ephesian two verse eight). That is the reason we can boldly say Jesus is the author of the amazing grace. He shed His blood on Calvary cross for our sins. By the way what does Calvary means? Dictionary declares Calvary is an open-air representation of the crucifixion of Jesus. The second definition: An experience of usually intense mental suffering.

Let us see our own definition of Calvary. There is a proverb in Creole says, "Pi ga ou fem montè Kalvè" which means do not try to give me trouble? Calvary is not a sweet word, it is not a comfortable position to be. But you know what Jesus was over there for you and me. The Bible says, "He came to that which was His own, but his own did not receive him. Yet to all who received him, to those who believed in his name, he gave there right to become children of God." Word became flesh and made his dwelling among us. (John one verse eleven-twelve and fourteen)

Thanks be to God our Heavenly Father who gave His only Son who died shamedly on the cross for our sins. He said whosoever believe shall not perish but have eternal life. I paraphrase John three sixteen.

Let me tell you something you don't have to pay to receive the amazing grace it is free of charge, Jesus paid the price on the Calvary cross for us. Just open your heart freely and received Him because He is the way, the truth and the life. Accept Him you will see how good He is. Amen!

Jesus is the truth Amazing Grace forever and ever.

Chapter Eleven

The Power of the Amazing Grace

Amazing grace is a nice title, by the way where it came from? As I said I had a dreamed and I saw "Amazing Grace writing in Heaven" it was very beautiful and after that I said let me write a book.

Jesus shed His blood on Calvary cross just to save us that is the reason He cried out "It is finished" why He said "It is finished" because in the old covenant period, there was a continual sacrifice for the atonement of sin. How? They had to kill an animal for their sins to be covered for example: bulls and goats were sacrificed. Therefore, it was not an easy time for the old covenant people. It's only cleansed the flesh, and such was and outside appearance. Therefore, it was a yearly demonstration, but thank God who send Jesus-Christ who shed His blood on Calvary cross to set us free from bondage.

The value of the blood – Without the blood of Jesus-Christ, it is impossible for us to have a personal relationship with God. After the disobedience of our first parents, there was a barrier draw between God and men because the first Adam had fallen into sin. God never makes mistake and that is the reason He sent us a second Adam, which is Jesus-Christ, His Son. The second Adam is the greatest there is no measurement on Him.

We have relationship with God through Jesus-Christ and by His word. Jesus said to the Samaritan woman, "Yet a time is coming and has now come when the true worshipers will worship the Father in Spirit and truth, for they are kind of worshipers the Father seeks. God is spirit, and his worshipers must worship in spirit and in truth"

(John four verses twenty-three and twenty-four) Amazing grace is a great thing we cannot really understand by the blood of Jesus Christ we can comprehend the value of the Amazing grace. Let us go a little bit further. Let us see the meaning of blood. The Lexicon Webster's Dictionary defines blood as "a fluid circulating throughout the vertebrate body, carrying nutrients and oxygen to the tissues and removing wastes and carbon dioxide."

The human body needs blood and water; without them, it is impossible for a human to be alive; especially without blood. Sometimes, individuals take a DNA test, and the result makes them happy or sad; even bring tears, depending on the result. I am telling you something there is no mistake in the blood of Jesus. We can say **He is our Father, He is our brother, He is our teacher, He is our doctor,** and we can shout proudly **He is everything to us.**

The blood of Jesus brings peace, the blood of Jesus brings hope, the blood of Jesus brings joy, the blood of Jesus brings life, the blood of Jesus brings salvation, which means we have been saved over two thousand years ago. That is the reason Jesus shouted on the cross before the Last word He said, "It is finished" I don't know if you understand the statement "it is finished" but for those who believed in the word of God "it is finished means a lot to us. "It is finished means no more deception, no more calamity no more sickness, no more death. Isaiah fifty-three verse five stated "But he was pierced for our transgressions, he was crushed for our iniquities; the punishment that brought us peace was upon him, **and by his wounds we are healed.** And John three verse sixteen declares "For God so loved the world that he gave his one and only son, that whoever believes in him shall not perish but have **eternal life.** That is the power of the amazing grace. If you believe in Jesus-Christ, we have the eternal life so therefore let us enjoy the power of Jesus-Christ because of His amazing grace. Enjoy "The Power of the Amazing Grace"

Poem
Amazing Grace

There is none like You Jesus Alone You are God

You shed Your blood for us On Calvary cross

Your love is unconditional

It is for whosoever believes

Whosoever means whosoever

Salvation is free

We do not need to pay any fee

The only fee we have to pay

Is to give our hearts to Him

That is the reason John three sixteen and seventeen stated For God so loved the world that he

Gave his one and only Son, that whoever believes in him shall not perish but have eternal life.

For God did not send his Son into the world to condemn the world, but to save the world through him.

Your color does not matter

Your race does not matter

Your language does not matter

Your background does not matter

Because heaven is for everyone who believe in Jesus-Christ of Nazareth. This is amazing. Isn't' it? Amazing grace that save a sinners like me.

Thank you God for Your precious gift, which is Jesus Christ of Nazareth.

Enjoy the Amazing Grace

Acrostic
Amazing Grace

Action on the Cross
Made my life forever through Him
Acknowledge Him as your Savior
Zion is His name through the blood
Immanuel is with us forever
Now let us rejoice
Great is our Lord
Gate of heaven is open for us
Redeemer and our comforter
Angels bow before His Presence
Christ is all in all
Eternally worship Him.

Chapter Seventeen

Hold on till the End

It is not easy to wait. So many people give up because they have been waiting for so many years nothing happen, we are truly understood because waiting is not a sweet moment. For example, when we are standing for a teller to call us, we are waiting because we know we are standing for good reason. Waiting to make deposit, waiting to cash check, or waiting to receive money, we are not going to give up because we are on the line for our good purpose.

There is a song wrote in Kréole title **"Ségnè menm nan liy nan déblokém"** In English "Lord, I am on the line deliver me," wrote by Brother Samuel Robuste. If we truly understand the song the writer wrote it because he is truly having a lot of faith in the Lord and our Savior.

Faith is the best key for a Christian to possess. Without faith it is impossible to serve the Lord. As a matter of fact, the world was made by the power of the word of faith. God said, "Let there be light" and at the same time there was light. According to the book of Genesis chapter one verse two. God spoke and thing happened. We are not on this earth by accident. God has a purpose for each and every one of us. The author of the book of Hebrew defines the word of faith. "Now faith is being sure of what we hope for and certain of what we do not see. (Hebrew eleven verse one.)

Faith is the key to accomplish anything in our lives. We can see faith walk with determination. If you go to school and wait until the term is over, surely, you are going to be graduated there is no lie about it. That it is faith and determination. But if you start and not finish you are not going to be graduate because automatically this or that person doesn't have faith and determination.

Someone said, "It is to be or not to be" Life is not easy. When we heard the news on television or radio most of them are not good, we feel discourage most of the time. Remember the Bible warned us about that. Jesus said to the disciples, "watch out that no one deceives you. For many will come in my name, claiming, "I am the Christ, and will deceive many. You will hear of wars and rumors of wars, but see to it that you are not alarmed. Such things must happen, but the end is still to come. Nation will rise against nation, and kingdom against kingdom. There will be famines and earthquakes in various places. All these are the beginning of birth pains. Matthew twenty-four verse four and eight.

As Christians, we are not going to be afraid because Jesus told the disciples to be ready for His coming and the news left for us as believers of Jesus-Christ. We are not going to give up instead we are going to be ready for His returned.

Jesus continued to speak to His disciples, "Therefore keep watch, because you do not know on what day your Lord will come. But understand this: if the owner of the house had known at what time of night the thief was coming, he would have kept watch and would not have let his house be broke into. So, you also must ready, because the Son of Man will come at an hour when you do not expect him. Matthew twenty-four verses forty-two and forty-four.

So therefore, be ready to meet our Lord and our Savior, remember, nothing is impossible to those who believe in Christ Jesus. **Don't give up, don't give up, and don't give up** because the promises of God are yes and amen. Our Christians motto is: **Hold on until the end.**

Monday, May 12, 2014, I had a revelation, I was saying: "Jesus is coming don't wait" I repeated that over and over until I woke up with my heart beaten the reason because I was saying that with a lot of energy, I woke up at seven o'clock in the morning. It is not a pleasure it is very serious.

Again, please get ready to meet our King of kings and the Lord of lords!

Chapter Eighteen

The New Jerusalem

Jerusalem is a beautiful place even though I do not go to visit yet, but they told me how wonderful it is and I agree. Where is he located? According to Jerusalem Wikipedia, the free encyclopedia – Jerusalem located on a plateau in the Judean Mountains between the Mediterranean and the Dead Sea is one of the oldest cities in the world. It is considered...

I remember there was a pastor he said the first country he must visit after he received his residence is Jerusalem that was his promise, and the dream came true. When he received the residence, he came to visit Jerusalem and brought a nice bag for me. There is a song title "Jerusalem" wrote by Paula Stefanovich:

Jerusalem, I want to walk your streets that are golden And I want to run where the angels have trod.

Jerusalem, I want to rest on the banks of your river in that city, city of God Jerusalem, Jerusalem

Sing for the nigh is o'er Hosanna in the highest

Hosanna forever, Forever more.

Jerusalem is real. Because of that he inspired us to write songs, poems and to visit why not because it is very meaningful.

Jerusalem is real. So many people like to visit almost every year even though it cost money. Remember the title of this specific subject is the New Jerusalem.

For us Christians, Jerusalem means a lot to us. Jerusalem is the place where Jesus is. Jerusalem is the City of God. Apostle of John said, "I saw the Holy City, the new Jerusalem, coming down out of heaven from God, prepared as a bride beautifully dressed for her husband. And I heard a loud voice from the throne saying, "now the dwelling of God is with men, and he will live with them. They will be his people, and God himself will be with them and be their God." (Revelation twenty-one verses two to three)

The revelation of John from God, so therefore the New Jerusalem is real. I want readers of the **"Amazing Grace"** realize one day we are not going to spend money to visit Jerusalem and buy a lot of good souvenirs for you and for others. As a matter of fact, the Jerusalem we know now for a lot of people is a place of business. Again, for us Christians, Jerusalem is a dwelling place of God. This New Jerusalem there will be no more vacation; there will be no more advertising, there will be no more business. There will be no more racism, there will be no more colors, there will be no more countries or nationalities, and there will be no more religions.

We are going to be united as brothers and sisters. Where the true love will be taking place, because Jesus will be sitting near to us that is The New Jerusalem. Therefore, let us starts The New Jerusalem while we are on this earth. How come? Starts love each other because Jesus is love. Without love it is impossible to enter in The New Jerusalem because Jesus is love. First John four verses seven and eight stated, Dear friends, let us love one another, for love comes from God. Everyone who loves has been born of God and knows God. Whoever does not love does not know God, because God is love.

Please enjoy the New Jerusalem

Chapter Nineteen

The Taste of Heaven

Definition of Taste According to dictionary is the sensation of flavor perceived in the mouth and throat on contact with a substance. But now, what is the definition of heaven. According to dictionary the place where God lives and where good people go after they die according to some religions: something that is very pleasant or good. The heavens: the sky…

According to Easy English Bible dictionary: Heaven the home of God.

Heaven the place the believers will live with Jesus, after they die.

Heaven is the best place for anyone live. But there is a condition it is not about religion, it is not about how great we are on our position that we have, it is not about how big we are, it is not about what kind of church we belong too. The only thing we have to do just accept Him as our personal Savior and Fried.

To start tasting heaven while we are on this earth, we need to have love in our heart for everyone, reason; without love it is impossible to go to heaven reason because Jesus is Love.

The gospel of John said, 'Dear friends, let us love one another, for love comes from God. Whoever does not love does not know God, because God is love.

This is how God showed his love among us: He sent his one and only Son into the world that we might live through Him. This is love; not that we loved God, but that he loved us and sent His Son as an atoning sacrifice for our sins. Dear friends, since God so loved us, we also ought to love one another. No one has ever seen God; but if we love one another, God lives in us, and his love is made complete in us. First John four verses seven to twelve.

God is love that is the reason love is eternal mean without end. The only thing we are going to have in heaven is love. In heaven there will be no sickness, there will be no death, there will be no will chair, there will be no blindness. We are going to see Jesus, as He is the only thing we are going to see is the marks on Jesus' hands just to remind us.

Let us taste heaven now.

The Quality of Heaven:
Heaven is **Precious**
Heaven is **Pure**
Heaven is **Pretty**
Heaven is **Perfect and**
Heaven is **Powerful**

We don't really have a specific word to describe heaven the only thing we have to do just prepare ourselves to meet our Heavenly Father and we will sing:

Heaven came down and glory filed my soul.
When at the cross my Savior made me whole:
My sins were washed away, and my night was turned to day.
Heaven came down and Glory filled my soul.
By John W. Peterson

Let us connect together in love because we are going to taste the heaven forever and ever in Jesus Mighty Precious Name.
Amen!

Chapter Twenty

Don't be Afraid

Afraid is not a strange word however let us see the meaning of it. Dictionary vocabulary .com Being afraid means you have a fear of something – and people are afraid of all sorts of things, from guns to ghost to being in arguments. People also say, "I'm afraid I have some bad news," which doesn't mean they're afraid of the news, but sorry that they have to share it. It's a similar situation for the saying "I'm afraid," which is a nice way of saying. "I'm sorry, but the answer is yes.

Jesus was comforted His Disciples by saying, "Do not let your hearts be troubled. Trust in God; trust also in me. In my Father's house are many mansions; if it were not so, I would have told you. I am going there to prepare a place for you, and if I go and prepare a place for you, I will come back and take you to be with me that you also may be where I am. (John chapter fourteen verse one to three) The reason Jesus said to His disciples may be where I am because If you accept Him as your personal Savior you will be with Him where He is but if you are not accept Him as Your personal Lord and Savior you will not be where He is. I make sure to clarify the word may be, all right.

Don't be afraid. You are very intelligent. Choose the best for your life. As I said before, there are a lot of bad things going on this earth. Now some people choose to get married with the same sex like man can choose a man or a woman can choose a woman to get married. And they choose to do that in church. I truly know man of God will not accept that in the church God gave him to lead. It is not about what people say but it is about what the Bible says which is the word of God. I know you are going to say that is the man words but is the inspiration of the Holy Spirit, which is the Father, the Son, and the Holy Spirit. The book of Genesis chapter one verse twenty-six 'Then God said, "God created man in his own image, in the image of God he created him; male and female he created them. God blessed them and said to them, "Be fruitful and increase in number; fill the earth and subdue it. Rule over the fish of the sea and the birds of the air and over every living creature that moves on the ground."

Let us see something, 'God said, "Be fruitful and increase in number, fill the earth and subdue it. How can we be fruitful with two man or two woman who choose to get married they cannot produce fruit. That is the reason when they do that they adopt children because they know they cannot have children. The only production they have the sins creation still going on. The children you adopt are adolescent they are going to do the same because you are they example. But God is a good God. If you change your mind and ask God to forgive you and if you accept Him as your personal Savior, He will do it. And Heaven is ready for you that is the reason I saw in the sky **"Amazing Grace"** **"Grace Infinie"**. There is none like Jesus.

We do have a lot of things going on, on this earth now, corruptions it is unbelievable it is not going to be better because the Bible is a book of truth. The book of Matthew chapter twenty-four tells us about the Signs of the End of the Age. Jesus said:" Watch out that no one deceives you. For many will come in my name, claiming, "I am the Christ, and will deceive many. You will hear of wars and rumors of wars but see to it that you are not alarmed. Such things must happen, but the end is still to come. Nation will rise against nation, and kingdom against kingdom. There will be famines and earthquakes in various places. All these are the beginnings of birth pains. (Matthew twenty-four verses four to eight)

As the title says: "Don't be afraid" God is a God of mercy, God is a God of compassion, God is a God of love. If you change your attitude and humble yourself before Him, you are going to see his miracles in your life. If you accept Jesus as your personal Savior and Lord, there will be no condemnation for you. The Word of God Says:

"Therefore, there is now no condemnation for those who are in Christ Jesus, because through Christ Jesus the law of the Spirit of life set me free from the law of sin and death. (Roman eighth verses one and two).

Don't be afraid because: God is good.

Jesus is on our side. He is our Mighty Power. He is pleading on our behalf before his Father for our sin's behavior. He is the King of kings and the Lord of Lords. He is our Best friend and He is the Alpha and Omega.

Don't be afraid.

Chapter Twenty-One

The Favor of God

W hat is favor? Dictionary.com defines favor is something done or granted out of goodwill, rather than from justice or for remuneration; a king act to ask favor.

Favor is really "Amazing Grace" The Bible declares for it is by grace you have been saved, through faith and this not from yourselves, it is the gift of God, not by works, so that no one can boast. For we are God's workmanship, created in Christ Jesus to do good works, which God prepared in advance for us to do. (Ephesian two verse eight and nine)

As Christians we need to meditate on favor every single minute in our lives, which is the goodness of the Lord, there is no other way to get save without the favor of God, the only way is to accept Him as your personal Savior, which is Jesus-Christ the Nazareth. Personally, I always think about the goodness of the Lord, the favor of God.

There is something I always admire in my heart Jesus never look at us as failure, there is no discrimination in Jesus, He loves us the way we are, if you are black He loves you, if you are white He loves you, if you are man He loves you, if you are woman He loves you, if you are educate He loves you, if you uneducated He loves you, wherever you came from He loves you. There is no discrimination at all in Jesus He is our true friend. The love of Jesus never fails. The only thing you have to do whatever mistakes you do just ask Him for forgiveness, and He will forgive you because He is a loving Father. I said there is no discrimination in Jesus there is no doubt about it but don't get me wrong if you choose to change your sex even, He loves you, but you make His heart unhappy. You are a man you choose to get a man to get married or if you are a woman, you choose a woman to get married and so many people give you license to do that it is wrong according to the Book of Genesis stated God created male and female which is Adam and Eve not Steve but Eve. (Genesis one verse twenty-seven)

God loves us so much He created us in His own image. Genesis said: "God created man in his own image, in the image of God he created him; male and female he created them. God blessed them and said to them, "Be fruitful and increase in number; fill the earth and subdue it. Rule over the fish of the sea and the birds of the air and over every living creature that moves on the ground." Genesis one verse twenty-seven and twenty-eight)

God is good if you want his favor to manifest for you, you need to stop the way you act and he will forgive you and then you will see the favor of God in your life.

May the Lord bless you. Please change your style and be real in Jesus Mighty Name. Enjoy the favor of God.

Chapter Twenty-Two

The Grace Promises

The promises of God are yes and amen. Reason, because he is a faithful God whatever He said He would do it. The story tells us God promised Abraham, Sarah going to have a child because of human nature Sarah was desperate because there was no way for Sarah to have a child because she was old enough for not to conceive and her husband as well. There was no doubt about that. Abraham was one hundred years old, and Sarah was ninety years old. Sarah was desperate he told her husband to go to her servant Hagar so perhaps you may conceive a child.

My ladies please be careful the Bible says Abraham was agreed in what is wife Sarai told him to do. The book of Genesis chapter sixteen verses one to six "The Lord has kept me from having children. Go, sleep with my maidservant; perhaps I can build a family through her." Abraham agreed to that Sarah said. So after Abram had been living in Canaan ten years, Sarai his wife took her Egyptian maidservant Hagar and gave her to her husband to be his wife.

He slept with Hagar, and she conceived. When she knew she was pregnant, she began to despise her mistress. Then Sarai said to Abram," You are responsible for the wrong I am suffering. I put my servant in your arms, and now that she knows she is pregnant, she despises me. May the Lord judge between you and me." Your servant is in your hands, "Abraham said. "Do with her whatever you think best." Then Sarai mistreated Hagar; so she fled from her.

I feel like to cry reason because of the amazing grace of God. God is very incomparable there is none like Him. Even though

Abraham and Sarah, I called them like this because later God change their names because of the faithfulness of God. His Promises remained to them. Three visitors came to Abraham "where is your wife, Sarah?" they asked him. "There, in the tent," he said. Then the Lord said, "I will surely returned to you about this time next year, and Sarah your wife will have a son." Now Sarah was listening at the entrance to the tent, which was behind him.

Abraham and Sarah were already old and well advanced in years, and Sarah was past the age of childbearing. So, Sarah laughed to herself as she thought. "After I am worn out and my master is old, will I now have this pleasure?" Then the Lord said to Abraham, "Why did Sarah laugh and say, "Will I really have a child, now that I am old?" Is anything too hard for the Lord? I will return to you at the appointed time next year and Sarah will have a son." "Sarah was afraid, so she lied and said," I did not laugh." But he said, "Yes, you did laugh." (Genesis chapter eighteen verses nine to fifteen)

Even though we are not faithful, but the promises of God are yes and amen. Faithfulness is the name of the Lord our God. He Never lie that is the reason God gave Abraham and Sarah Isaac was a promise child in French **"Enfant de la Promesse"** Isaac means **laughter** because his mother was laughing. The promises of God will be with us forever. The promises of God are yes and amen.

So therefore, stay focus on the promises of God.

Chapter Twenty-Three

Personal Testimony

Before I finish writing "Amazing Grace" I would like to give my special testimony, just to let you know how great God is. When I was a child, I saw my sister and my brother going to school and other children has well and I said to my father I want to go to school and he said to me, "you are too small to go to school." I did not stop telling him the same thing over and over. Has I said before my father did not born in Haiti but he was born in Santo Domingo and when he was about twenty he came to Haiti and met my mother. When I was nine years old my father went back to Santo Domingo.

My Grandmother her name was Silamante Noel, which is my father's mother said okay now I am going to send you to school. Now even though my grandmother did not know how to read but she was very intelligent for example: whenever she saw something writing in a board wherever it is you have to read it for her, and you have to read it properly for her. She was very smart in so many ways. She died when she was eighty-six years old.

There was a teacher in my community where I was living. That man was assembling a lot of children at his house doing school for them. That is the place my grandmother was sending me. There was a funny story behind that. When the teacher making a fart, he told us to tell him sorry any time he made a fart we have to tell him sorry but me, I never tell him sorry, and I said to my grandmother I am not going to that school anymore. My grandmother sends me to a normal school. The reason I shared that to all my readers is because I want you to know whatever God wants you to become, He will do it because He is great. Our future

Are in His Mighty Hands. My story is very amazing really; you might see it is very funny whatever you say it's okay. God has a plan for each and every one of us. The same way he had plan for Jeremiah the Prophet. For I know the plans I have for you," declares the Lord, "plans to prosper you and not to harm you, plans to give you hope and a future. To give hope (Jeremiah twenty-nine verse eleven)

Don't be discouraged but keep it up you can make it in Jesus Mighty Name. Whatever you have in mind to do just do it don't say you cannot in the dictionary of man we can see the negative word cannot but in the Dictionary of God you will never see the negative word you cannot but you will see the positive word you can because God is a God of miracle where there is no way He will make a way because He is the same yesterday, today and forever. That is the "Amazing Grace"

Let me give you another story about my childhood. My mother told me when I was about four years old, the place I was living there was a man who was a voodoo man he had in mind to kill a lot of children in that neighborhood. There were five children in that place, and I was one of them. The man killed three of them and the two he could not kill them. My mother said to me I became very sick I could not eat and had a strong fever never stop she said the only thing I drink just only sour tea everyday. One day my mother told me she was sleeping, and he saw the voodoo man came in front of her bed with a bottle in his hand he said to her I bring you your child soul I don't want her anymore. And my mother said to me, I was sneezing three times and I way cup.

The reason I share that to you my readers because I want to let you know that, devil is a liar. He can attack the children of God but good news he cannot kill them because God has plan for each and every one of us. Devil cannot kill the plan of God my mother told me I started preaching when I was about four years old even though I did not know anything, but the Holy Spirit was in me sometimes when I connected in the Internet I saw children preaching the gospel of Jesus-Christ and whenever I saw that my eyes turned to tears because I remember my story. Parents do not discourage your child or your children whatever you see in them help them to develop the gifts God placed in them. You might have a nurse you don't know. You might have a medical doctor, but you don't know. You might have a lawyer you don't know. You might have a schoolteacher you don't know; you might have a pastor you don't know, you might have an evangelist you don't know as a matter of fact I am an evangelist now so therefore never turn off the gift that you see on your child or children.

As I said before devil is a liar because he is the author of lie. Don't give up on your dream keep it up until you reach your goal.

God is good all the time and all the time God is good.

Please enjoy "The Amazing Grace"

Chapter Twenty-Four

The Reality of Grace

W hat is the meaning of reality? Dictionary defines reality as the quality or state of being actual or true or resemblance to what is real.

The reality of grace is Jesus Christ of Nazareth. The reality of grace is John three sixteen for God so loved the world he gave His only Son whosoever believes in Him shall not perish but have everlasting life. We don't have anything to do or anything to add because Jesus took control of it. Ephesians says it is by grace you have been saved, through faith – and this not from yourselves, it is the gift of God, not by works, so that no one can boast. Ephesian two verse eight and nine.

We are talking about of "The Reality of Grace" it is a little bit complex for so many people because they try to add a lot of things behind the truth reason because of lack of knowledge according to Hosea four verse six "My people are destroyed from lack of knowledge" it is not other people, but it is God's people. That is the reason we do have a lot of doctrines some are real and some are false but no matter what, I have good news for you the doctrine of Jesus-Christ is the true one you don't have to wear white all the time to get the reality of grace, you don't have to do fifty days or one hundred and fifty days to get the reality of grace because Jesus said on the cross before His last word He said" "It is finished" (John nineteen verse thirty) what is the meaning of it is finished? The meaning of it is finished means "is it is finish" we don't have to add anything to get save we do get saved through the blood of Jesus Christ.

The word of God continues to say, Yet to all who received him, to those who believed in his name, he gave the right to become children of God. Children born not of natural descent, nor of human decision or a husband's will, but born of God. (John one verse twelve and thirteen) I don't want to speak by myself but I want the Holy Spirit to guide me so I can understand the reality of grace so you will understand and be blessed as well.

Ephesian two verse eight and nine stated "For it is by grace you have been saved, through faith and this not from yourselves, it is the gift of God not by works, so that no one can boast." Salvation is a gift from God so therefore it is just to accept Jesus-Christ as your personal Savior and friend we do not have to do a lot of decorations or demonstrations to get save.

Don't let anyone full you just read the word of God and you will be saved. Roman ten verse nine says: "If you confess with your mouth, "Jesus is Lord," and believe in your heart that God raised him from the dead, you will be saved." So therefore, confess it with your mouth you will be saved and after that get a church to go and you will see how bless you are. You don't have anything to pay or to do to get save Jesus already paid the price on Calvary cross, He shed His blood they were humiliated Him on the cross just for me and for you.

No one can destroy the reality of grace. When Jesus was born king Herod heard about it he sent the Magi secretly and found out from them the exact time the star had appeared. He sent them on Bethlehem and said, 'Go and make a careful search for the child. As soon as you find him, report to me, so that I too may go and worship him." That is a big lie. After they had heard the king, they went on their way, and the star they had seen in the east went ahead when they saw the star, they were overjoyed. On coming the house, they saw the child with his mother Mary, and they bowed down and worshiped him. Then they opened their treasures and presented him with gifts of gold and of incense and of myrrh. And having been warned in a dream not to go back to Herod, they returned to their country by another route. (Matthew two verses seven through twelve)

No one can destroy the Reality of grace. Just take a time to think about your life without the reality of grace you will not be alive today just because of Jesus-Christ of Nazareth you are here on this earth. God is good just remember the story of the Apostle Paul he was a blasphemer and God changed him to become a believer he wrote more books in the New Testament twelve or thirteen according to the Theologians report.

David was and adulterer and murdered and God transformed him as a man after God's own heart. Act thirteen verse twenty-two David wrote about Seventy-three Psalms. He humbled himself before God he wrote Psalm fifty-one after he committed adultery with Bathsheba. God forgave him. David teaches us a lot of lessons about that we need to follow his example. God is a God of forgiveness. First word of Jesus on the cross "Father, forgive them for they do not know what they do." (Gospel of Luke chapter twenty-three verse thirty-four)

There is another story the Samaritan woman. The Bible says, "Jacob's well was there, and Jesus was tired as he was from the journey, sat down by the well. It was about the sixth hour. When a Samaritan woman came to draw water, Jesus said to her, "Will you give me a drink?" His disciples had gone into the town to buy food. The Samaritan woman said to Him, "You are a Jew, and I am a Samaritan woman. How can you ask me for a drink? For Jews do not associate with Samaritans. Jesus answered her, "If you knew the gift of God and who it is that asks you for a drink, you would have asked him and he would have given you living water." She answered, "Sir," You have nothing to draw with and the well is deep. Where can you get this living water? Are you greater than our father Jacob, who gave us the well and drank from it himself, as did also his sons and his flocks and herds?" my comment is: "The Samaritan woman heard about Jesus but she did not know who He is personally. Jesus answered, "Everyone who drinks this water will be thirsty again, but whoever drinks the water I give him will never thirst. Indeed, the water I give him will become in him a spring of water welling up to eternal life."

The woman said to Him, "Sir, give me this water so that I won't get thirsty and have to keep coming here to draw water."

The Samaritan woman had something else in her mind for Jesus again, she did not know who Jesus is all about. He told her, "Go, call your husband and come back." "I have no husband." She replied.

Jesus said to her, "You are right when you say you have no husband. The fact is, you have had five husbands, and the man you now have is not your husband. What you have just said is quite true."

The Samaritan woman was trying to full Jesus, but no one can full Him, no matter who we are we cannot full Jesus of Nazareth. It is a nice, wonderful story but let me tell you the Samaritan Woman changed her lifestyle she was a prostitute, and she became an evangelist by saying "He told me everything I ever did." Because of her testimony many of the Samaritans from that town believed in Jesus. Came from the Gospel of John Chapter four.

Your lifestyle can change too as well because of the reality of grace.

No one can destroy the reality of grace.

Chapter Twenty-Five

Rejoice Forever

Amazing to come to an end; it is a nice subject you know the last chapter is "Rejoice forever" but what rejoice means, as you know I love to go to definition of the words. According to Merriam-Webster dictionary, Rejoice is to feel or show that you are very happy about something. The second definition from King James Version Dictionary definition: Rejoice is to experience joy and gladness in a high degree; to be exhilarated with lively and pleasurable sensations; to exult.

What about forever definition: According to dictionary.com Forever: It is without ever <u>ending</u>, <u>eternally</u>; to <u>last forever</u>.

The song I mentioned earlier in the book: Written by Eliza Edmunds Hewitt (1851-1920)

"When we all get to heaven,

What a day of rejoicing that will be!

When we all see Jesus,

We will sing and shout the victory."

Onward to the prize before us!

Soon His beauty we'll behold;

Soon the pearly gates will open;

We shall tread the streets of gold.

The song has four verses, but I love the last verse so much because I know there is no joke about that one-day we are going to be with Jesus forever. We will sing and shout the victory!

That is our hope. In heaven there will be no more sickness, no more misery, no more trouble, no more death because Jesus said on the cross "It is finished".

There is another powerful song wrote by Haldor Lillenas (1885-1959) Stated:

Wonderful grace of Jesus, greater than all my sin;

How shall my tongue describe it,

Where shall its praise begin?

For the wonderful grace of Jesus reaches me!

The chorus says: Wonderful the matchless grace of Jesus,

Deeper than the mighty rolling sea;

Higher than the mountain, sparkling like a fountain,

Broader than the scope of my transgressions.

O grâce Merveilleuse, don qui nous vient de Dieu

Grâce si précieuse, Fleuve jaillit des cieux

Qui donc saurait décrire sa force et sa fraîcheur

Et qui donc a pu dire Quelle est sa profondeur.

Nous n'avons qu'un seul sujet de gloire,

C'est ta sainte croix, divin Sauveur

Ta grace est puissante, toute suffisante,

Et ton sang nous rend plus que vainqueur.

Plus touchant que l'hymne des archanges

Est le chant qu'entonnent les élus,

Venez, chrétiens, qu'éclatent vos louanges:

Gloire à Jésus.

I put the song in two languages: English and French just for the benefit of those who speak French and remember I told you I had a vision I saw in heaven "Amazing grace and Grace Infinie". That is the reason I write the book. If you don't have Jesus as your personal Savior say Lord, I know I am a sinner but I know as well you shed your blood on Calvary cross for my sin please Lord receive me as your child thank you Lord for saving my soul. It you repeat those words you are save and go to a Christian church near you. Please enjoy the Amazing Grace of Jesus-Christ.

AMAZING GRACE REJOICE

www.ingramcontent.com/pod-product-compliance
Lightning Source LLC
Chambersburg PA
CBHW051239120626
46547CB00014B/1711